THE OFFICIAL
ENGLAND
ANNUAL 2025

Written by Andy Greeves
Designed by Chris Dalrymple

A Grange Publication

CONTENTS

WELCOME TO THE OFFICIAL ENGLAND ANNUAL 2025

**As the lyrics of one of England's unofficial anthems
(Neil Diamond's *Sweet Caroline*) goes, 'good times never seemed so good'...**

Those words have certainly rung true following both the Three Lions and the Lionesses in recent years.

In the Official England Annual 2025, we look back on Gareth Southgate's wonderful 102-match tenure in charge of the Three Lions, which produced so many sporting highs. This included a run to the final of back-to-back to European Championships and the story of the most recent of those - UEFA Euro 2024 - can be found overleaf.

Ahead of UEFA Women's Euro 2025, we check in with Sarina Wiegman's Lionesses, who are reigning European Champions of course. We also take a look at how the England teams of tomorrow are shaping up with our youth teams review and find out how the Para Lions fared at the 2024 Deaf Euros in Turkey.

Elsewhere, there are other features, quizzes, games and plenty more besides to entertain England fans of all ages!

Enjoy the 2025 Annual and COME ON ENGLAND!

COME ON ENGLAND
#ThreeLions #Lionesses

UEFA EURO 2024 REVIEW

HISTORY MAKERS

At UEFA Euro 2024, the Three Lions made history as the first England Men's team to make it to the final of a major tournament on foreign soil. Let's look back on a memorable campaign in Germany in the summer of 2024…

SERBIA 0-1 ENGLAND

UEFA Euro 2024 - Group C
16 June 2024
Arena AufSchalke, Gelsenkirchen

England kicked off their Euro 2024 campaign with victory over Serbia in Group C. Jude Bellingham's header after just 13 minutes in Gelsenkirchen proved the difference between the two sides as Serbia pushed the Three Lions hard throughout the match.

Former Fulham and Newcastle United striker Aleksandar Mitrović saw an early effort go just wide and Jordan Pickford was called into action late on, tipping Dušan Vlahović 's shot over the bar to maintain his clean sheet.

Harry Kane had the best chance to double England's lead when he got onto the end of a Jarrod Bowen cross, but Serbia goalkeeper Predrag Rajković pulled off a fine save.

ENGLAND: Pickford, Walker, Rice, Stones, Guéhi, Saka (Bowen 76), Alexander-Arnold (Gallagher 69), Kane, Bellingham (Mainoo 86), Foden, Trippier

DENMARK 1-1 ENGLAND

UEFA Euro 2024 - Group C
20 June 2024
Frankfurt Arena, Frankfurt

The Three Lions were held to a 1-1 draw by Denmark in their second group game. Harry Kane broke the deadlock on 18 minutes when he finished from close range after Kyle Walker raced down the wing to pounce on a defensive lapse by the Danes and his cross found the England captain.

 Denmark worked their way back into the contest and Morten Hjulmand equalised with a powerful shot from 25 yards out just before the half hour mark. Phil Foden hit the post in the second half and Jordan Pickford had to get down quickly to stop another long-range effort from Hjulmund as both sides had to settle for a share of the spoils.

ENGLAND: Pickford, Walker, Rice, Stones, Guéhi, Saka (Eze 69), Alexander-Arnold (Gallagher 54), Kane (Watkins 69), Bellingham, Foden (Bowen 69), Trippier

ENGLAND 0-0 SLOVENIA

UEFA Euro 2024 - Group C
25 June 2024
Cologne Stadium, Cologne

A goalless draw with Slovenia saw England finish top of Group C to progress to the knockout stage of the competition. The England side dominated possession in the first half, and they did have the ball in the net on 20 minutes but Phil Foden was ruled to have been just offside before sliding the ball across to Bukayo Saka who tapped it in.

The Three Lions continued to cause problems for the Slovenian defence in the second half but they were unable to find a breakthrough.

ENGLAND: Pickford, Walker, Rice, Stones, Guéhi, Saka (Palmer 71), Kane (Gallagher 105), Bellingham (Konsa 105), Foden (Gordon 89), Trippier (Alexander-Arnold 85), Gallagher (Mainoo 46)

Final Group C Table

		P	W	D	L	GF	GA	GD	PTS
1	England (Q)	3	1	2	0	2	1	+1	5
2	Denmark (Q)	3	0	3	0	2	2	0	3
3	Slovenia (Q)	3	0	3	0	2	2	0	3
4	Serbia	3	0	2	1	1	2	-1	2

ENGLAND 2-1 SLOVAKIA
(after extra-time)
UEFA Euro 2024 - Round of 16
30 June 2024
Arena AufSchalke, Gelsenkirchen

With 90 seconds remaining on the clock at Arena AufSchalke, it looked like England were heading home at the hands of Slovakia. But a moment of magic from Jude Bellingham sparked a dramatic turnaround for the Three Lions.

The Real Madrid star pulled off a sensational overhead kick in the 95th minute to cancel out Ivan Schranz's first-half strike and take the round of 16 game to extra-time. Just 52 seconds into that extra 30 minutes, Harry Kane headed home from Ivan Toney's flick-on to give England victory and a place in the final eight.

ENGLAND: Pickford, Walker, Rice, Stones, Guéhi, Saka, Kane (Gallagher 105), Bellingham (Konsa 105), Foden (Toney 90+5), Trippier (Palmer 66), Mainoo (Eze 84)

SWITZERLAND 1-1 ENGLAND
(after extra-time - England win 5-3 on penalties)
UEFA Euro 2024 - Quarter-final
6 July 2024
Düsseldorf Arena, Düsseldorf

Following a cagey first half, Breel Embolo had given Switzerland the lead after 75 minutes of the match in Düsseldorf. England found the equaliser just five minutes later as Saka fired home a fine left-footed shot to force extra-time. Both teams had chances in the extra 30 minutes but neither could find the all-important winner. With the score level at 1-1 after extra-time, the game went to penalties.

Jordan Pickford saved Manuel Akanji's effort while Cole Palmer, Jude Bellingham, Bukayo Saka, Ivan Toney and Trent Alexander-Arnold all stepped up and despatched five perfect spot-kicks to book the Three Lions' place in the final four of the competition.

ENGLAND: Pickford, Walker, Rice, Stones, Saka, Kane (Toney 109), Bellingham, Foden (Alexander-Arnold 115), Trippier (Shaw 78), Konsa (Eze 78), Mainoo (Palmer 78)

ENGLAND 2-1 NETHERLANDS
UEFA Euro 2024 - Semi-Final
10 July 2024
BVB Stadion, Dortmund

'Ollie, Ollie, Ollie… Oi, Oi, Oi…' That was the chant ringing out in Dortmund – not to mention living rooms and pubs across England - as the final whistle was blown on the Three Lions' semi-final against the Netherlands, after substitute Ollie Watkins scored a 90th-minute winner to send his side into the final.

The Dutch opened the scoring after just seven minutes of the semi-final when a long-range effort from winger Xavi Simons flew past Jordan Pickford and into the top corner. England equalised 11 minutes later through a Harry Kane penalty after VAR looked into a late challenge by Denzel Dumfries on the Three Lions captain.

England continued to push for a second with Phil Foden hitting the woodwork and Bukayo Saka's strike was ruled out due to provider Kyle Walker being offside. With 90 minutes on the clock, Watkins received a pass from fellow substitute Cole Palmer which saw him turn and drill the ball into the bottom left corner to secure a 2-1 victory.

ENGLAND: Pickford, Walker, Rice, Stones, Guéhi, Saka (Konsa 90+3), Kane (Watkins 80), Bellingham, Foden (Palmer 80), Trippier (Shaw 46), Mainoo (Gallagher 90+3)

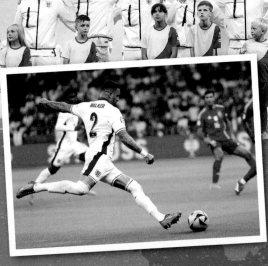

SPAIN 2-1 ENGLAND

UEFA Euro 2025 - Final
14 July 2024
Olympiastadion, Berlin

As had been the case at the delayed UEFA Euro 2020, there was heartbreak for the Three Lions in the final. Three years after finishing as runners-up to Italy, the England side went down 2-1 to Spain in front of a crowd of 65,600 at Berlin's Olympiastadion.

Nico Williams put the Spanish ahead early in the second half before Jude Bellingham laid the ball off for substitute Cole Palmer who fired it into the bottom corner for England's equaliser on 73 minutes. Cue pandemonium in the stands, where Three Lions fans greatly outnumbered their opponents.

Southgate's men pushed for a winner but Spain soaked up the pressure and with just four minutes of normal time remaining Mikel Oyarzabal stabbed home from a Marc Cucurella cross to make it 2-1.

Declan Rice had a chance at the other end, heading towards goal from a corner, but Spain's goalkeeper Unai Simón parried his effort, and Dani Olmo headed Marc Guéhi's follow-up off the line as time ran out for England and Spain secured their fourth European Championship title.

ENGLAND: Pickford, Walker, Shaw, Rice, Stones, Guéhi, Saka, Kane (Watkins 61), Bellingham, Foden (Toney 89), Mainoo (Palmer 70)

THANK YOU GARETH SOUTHGATE!

Given the success he enjoyed as England manager, it seemed fitting that Gareth Southgate's 102nd and last match in charge of the national team would come in a major tournament final. Alas, a 2-1 defeat to Spain in the UEFA Euro 2024 showpiece match denied Southgate the ultimate fairytale finish, but what a journey it had been for England with the former Crystal Palace, Aston Villa and Middlesbrough player at the helm...

Capped 57 times for England as a player between 1995 and 2004, Southgate took charge of the England MU21s in 2013 and oversaw 37 matches as head coach. He was appointed as interim manager of the senior team in September 2016 and got off to a winning start with a 2-0 triumph over Malta in a 2018 FIFA World Cup qualifier at Wembley Stadium the following month.

Appointed as manager on a permanent basis in November 2016, Southgate guided the Three Lions to the 2018 FIFA World Cup Finals. The tournament was a memorable one, as his side became the first England men's team to reach a World Cup semi-final since Sir Bobby Robson's class of 1990. Along the way, they won their first-ever penalty shootout at the tournament against Colombia in the round of 16, en route to eventually finishing fourth at that summer's competition.

The delayed UEFA Euro 2020 saw Southgate's side go one step further as they became the first England men's team since Sir Alf Ramsey's World Cup winners of 1966 to reach a major tournament final. There were magical moments along the way, including a 2-0 defeat of Germany in the round of 16, a 4-0 quarter-final triumph against Ukraine and a 2-1 extra-time victory over Denmark in the semi-final before the agony of a penalty shootout loss to Italy in the Final.

England's third qualification for a major tournament with Southgate as manager came as the Three Lions made it to the 2022 FIFA World Cup, with results in qualifying including a 10-0 away win in San Marino. Southgate's side topped Group B at the finals with wins over Iran and Wales and a draw with the United States, and they saw off Senegal in the round of 16. But they exited the competition after a 2-1 defeat to France in the quarter-finals.

England went unbeaten during the calendar year of 2023, during which time qualification to UEFA Euro 2024 was secured with two matches remaining. In the tournament finals, England topped Group C with a win over Serbia and draws with Denmark and Slovenia. An extra-time victory over Slovakia in the round of 16 was followed by a penalty shootout triumph against Switzerland in the quarter-finals. Substitute Ollie Watkins' late winner against the Netherlands in the semi-finals took England to a second consecutive European Championships Final.

Southgate leaves quite a legacy. His 102 games as senior team manager combined with his 57 caps as a player means he has been involved in more England Men's Internationals (159) than anyone else in history.

LEE CARSLEY

Following Gareth Southgate's departure as England manager, Lee Carsley was appointed as England Men's interim head coach ahead of the start of the 2024-25 UEFA Nations League campaign.

Carsley stepped up from his role in charge of the MU21s, for the fixtures away to Republic of Ireland and at home to Finland in September 2024, with a view to remaining in the position throughout autumn while the FA's recruitment process for a new permanent head coach continued.

Carsley had been England MU21 head coach since July 2021 and, in 2023, led the Young Lions to a first UEFA U21 European Championship success since 1984. Prior to that, Carsley held various coaching roles across England's development teams and was briefly in charge of the MU20s.

PLAYER PROFILES

(H) Home (A) Away (N) Neutral Venue
Information correct as of August 2024

JORDAN PICKFORD

Legacy Number: 1225
Position: Goalkeeper
Date/Place of Birth: 7 March 1994 – Washington, England
England Debut: 10 November 2017 v Germany (H)

An ever-present at UEFA Euro 2024 - where he won his 68th cap in the final of the competition - Jordan's impressive form in Germany saw him keep a record 11th clean sheet for the Three Lions in a major international tournament, as they drew 0-0 with Slovenia in the group stage. Jordan thrives in penalty shootouts and at Euro 2024 his save to deny Manuel Akanji of Switzerland helped his nation progress to the semi-finals of the tournament.

AARON RAMSDALE

Legacy Number: 1265
Position: Goalkeeper
Date/Place of Birth: 14 May 1998 – Chesterton
England Debut: 15 November 2021 v San Marino (A)

Aaron travelled to Germany as part of the England squad for Euro 2024. Such a positive influence around the camp, Gareth Southgate selected Aaron for friendlies against Scotland in September 2023 and against Iceland in June 2024, which brought his senior England caps tally to five.

SAM JOHNSTONE

Legacy Number: 1262
Position: Goalkeeper
Date/Place of Birth: 25 March 1993 – Preston
England Debut: 6 June 2021 v Romania (H)

At the time of writing, Sam had never conceded a goal while playing for England's senior side. The shot stopper won his fourth cap - and his first in more than two years - in a friendly victory over Australia in October 2023. That summer, he'd also been selected for the Three Lions' squad for UEFA Euro 2024 qualifiers against Malta and North Macedonia, but unfortunately wasn't available for the tournament finals in Germany through injury.

DEAN HENDERSON

Legacy Number: 1257
Position: Goalkeeper
Date/Place of Birth: 12 March 1997 – Whitehaven
England Debut: 12 November 2020 v Republic of Ireland (H)

Dean was one of three goalkeepers selected for England's squad for Euro 2024 but, along with Aaron Ramsdale, he didn't get a look in due to Jordan Pickford's scintillating form. After representing the Three Lions at U16, U17, U20 and U21 level, Dean made his senior debut as a substitute in a 3-0 friendly victory over the Republic of Ireland at Wembley Stadium in November 2020 – his only cap at the time of writing.

KYLE WALKER

Legacy Number: 1178
Position: Defender
Date/Place of Birth: 28 May 1990 – Sheffield
England Debut: 12 November 2011 v Spain (H)

Kyle featured in every one of England's seven games en route to the final of Euro 2024, winning his 90th cap in the showpiece match against Spain. The full-back has been a key player in the Three Lions' defence over the years with his speed and strength making him a tough opponent. Since making his Man of the Match debut against Sweden in 2011, Kyle has represented his country at five major tournaments and reached two European Championship finals.

JOHN STONES

Legacy Number: 1202
Position: Defender
Date/Place of Birth: 28 May 1994 – Barnsley
England Debut: 30 May 2014 v Peru (H)

John has played an integral role in the England team at their last four major tournaments – the 2018 and 2022 FIFA World Cups and Euro 2020 and 2024. He played every minute of every match in Germany in the summer of 2024 to bring his caps tally to 79. The centre-back has also netted three times for his country, including a brace in a 6-1 win over Panama in the group stage of the 2018 World Cup.

HARRY MAGUIRE

Legacy Number: 1223
Position: Defender
Date/Place of Birth: 5 March 1993 – Sheffield
England Debut: 8 October 2017 v Lithuania (A)

A mainstay of England squads under former Head Coach Gareth Southgate, Harry missed out on a place at Euro 2024 due to injury. In his last tournament appearance, the 2022 World Cup, Harry's impressive performances earned him a place in the Team of the Tournament. He had received the same recognition at UEFA Euro 2020 after playing in the last group game and all of England's knockout matches. The experienced defender - who has netted seven times for his country at the time of writing - earnt his 63rd cap in a friendly against Brazil in March 2024.

KIERAN TRIPPIER

Legacy Number: 1222
Position: Defender
Date/Place of Birth: 19 September 1990 – Bury
England Debut: 13 June 2017 v France (A)

Kieran won his 54th England cap in their Euro 2024 semi-final triumph over the Netherlands after featuring in all of the Three Lions' games up to that point in the tournament. The right-back was named in the Team of the Tournament for his performances at the 2018 World Cup and he was also in the England squads for Euro 2020, where he played three games including the final against Italy, and the 2022 World Cup. Since Euro 2024 he has announced his retirement from international football.

LUKE SHAW

Legacy Number: 1201
Position: Defender
Date/Place of Birth: 12 July 1995 – Kingston upon Thames
England Debut: 5 March 2014 v Denmark (H)

Luke started England's 2024 European Championship final against Spain after fighting to get back to full fitness following an injury that sidelined him in February 2024. The Manchester United left-back also played a part in the Three Lions' quarter and semi-finals en route to the showpiece match in Berlin. Luke has been involved in the senior England set-up for more than a decade with 34 caps and three goals at the time of writing – his most memorable coming against Italy in the final of Euro 2020.

MARC GUÉHI

Legacy Number: 1268
Position: Defender
Date/Place of Birth: 13 July 2000 – Abidjan, Cote d'Ivoire
England Debut: 26 March 2022 v Switzerland (H)

Marc started in six of England's seven matches at Euro 2024 during which he completed a total of 415 passes, made seven blocks and won four tackles as well as making seven clearances. The central defender played a big part in the Three Lions reaching the tournaments finals, as he featured in five qualifying matches.

JARRAD BRANTHWAITE

Legacy Number: 1281
Position: Defender
Date/Place of Birth: 27 June 2002 – Carlisle
England Debut: 3 June 2024 v Bosnia and Herzegovina (H)

Standing 6ft 5in tall, Jarrad moved from Carlisle United to Everton in 2020 and was a KNVB Cup winner during a loan spell with PSV Eindhoven during the 2022-23 season. Previously capped at U20 and U21 levels, Jarrad was included in Gareth Southgate's provisional squad for UEFA Euro 2024 and made his debut as a substitute in the 3-0 friendly victory over Bosnia and Herzegovina at St. James' Park, Newcastle prior to the tournament.

LEVI COLWILL

Legacy Number: 1274

Position: Defender

Date/Place of Birth: 26 February 2003 – Southampton

England Debut: 13 October 2023 v Australia (H)

A product of Chelsea's academy, Levi impressed during loan spells with Huddersfield Town in 2021-22 and Brighton & Hove Albion the following season. The defender won the Syrenka Cup with England U17s in 2019 before going on to represent the Young Lions at U19 and U21 level and stepping up to the senior group in 2023.

RICO LEWIS

Legacy Number: 1277

Position: Defender

Date/Place of Birth: 21 November 2004 – Bury

England Debut: 20 November 2023 v North Macedonia (A)

A product of Manchester City's famed youth academy, Rico made his Cityzens debut against AFC Bournemouth in a Premier League match in August 2022 and quickly established himself as an important member of their first team squad. Capped by England between U16 and U21 level, Rico's senior debut for the Three Lions came when he started in the 1-1 draw in North Macedonia aged just 18 years, 11 months and 29 days at the time.

EZRI KONSA

Legacy Number: 1279

Position: Defender

Date/Place of Birth: 23 October 1997 – London

England Debut: 23 March 2024 v Brazil (H)

Ezri fitted seamlessly into England's starting back-three for their Euro 2024 quarter-final against Switzerland. He also featured twice as a substitute at the tournament, coming on as an extra-time swap for Jude Bellingham in the round of 16 victory over Slovakia, while he replaced Bukayo Saka late on against the Netherlands.

LEWIS DUNK

Legacy Number: 1238

Position: Defender

Date/Place of Birth: 21 November 1991 – Brighton

England Debut: 15 November 2018 v United States (H)

Lewis became just the fourth Brighton & Hove Albion player to earn a senior cap for England when he debuted in the 3-0 win over the United States in November 2018. A near-five year wait for his next cap followed until he started in the 3-1 away win in Scotland in September 2023. During the 2023-24 season, he also featured in friendlies against Australia, Brazil, Belgium and Bosnia and Herzegovina and was named in Gareth Southgate's 26-man squad for Euro 2024.

BEN CHILWELL

Legacy Number: 1235

Position: Defender

Date/Place of Birth: 21 December 1996 – Milton Keynes

England Debut: 11 September 2018 v Switzerland (H)

Ben's start in England's 2-2 draw with Belgium at Wembley Stadium in March 2024 brought his senior international caps tally to 21. The defender was part of the Three Lions' squad for Euro 2020 while he also started in the UEFA Nations League semi-final against the Netherlands back in June 2019.

FIKAYO TOMORI

Legacy Number: 1246

Position: Defender

Date/Place of Birth: 19 December 1997 – Calgary, Canada

England Debut: 17 November 2019 v Kosovo (A)

Born in Canada to Nigerian parents, Fikayo had the option of representing a number of countries at international level. Having moved to England as a toddler and been raised in Kent, he opted to play for the Three Lions from U19 to senior level, having previously played for Canada U20s. Fikayo had been capped five times by England as of August 2024.

JOE GOMEZ

Legacy Number: 1228

Position: Defender

Date/Place of Birth: 23 May 1997 – London

England Debut: 10 November 2017 v Germany (H)

Previously capped by England between U16 and U21 level, Joe made the transition to senior international football look easy. He played 75 minutes and helped keep a clean on his debut against Germany in November 2017 before being named Man of the Match in his second Three Lions appearance that same month as he helped nullify the attacking threat of the likes of Neymar, Gabriel Jesus and Philippe Coutinho in a goalless draw with Brazil.

TRENT ALEXANDER-ARNOLD

Legacy Number: 1233

Position: Midfielder

Date/Place of Birth: 7 October 1998 – Liverpool

England Debut: 7 June 2018 v Costa Rica (H)

Having previously operated at full-back/wing-back, Trent demonstrated his versatility at Euro 2024 by also operating in a midfield role. He featured in four matches at the tournament and memorably, came off the bench to score the winning penalty in the quarter-final shootout against Switzerland in Düsseldorf. That was his ninth and final England appearance of the 2023-24 season, bringing his caps international caps tally to 29, while his goal against Bosnia and Herzegovina in June 2024 was his third in an England shirt.

COLE PALMER

Legacy Number: 1276

Position: Midfielder

Date/Place of Birth: 06 May 2002 – Manchester

England Debut: 17 November 2023 v Malta (H)

Cole was most definitely an 'impact substitute' for England at Euro 2024. He supplied the assist for fellow sub Ollie Watkins' winner in the semi-final against the Netherlands then came off the bench to finish off a fine move to draw the Three Lions level in the final versus Spain. The forward completed 52 passes in his 144 minutes of action at the tournament and made 10 dribbles and four runs into key play areas.

JORDAN HENDERSON

Legacy Number: 1170
Position: Midfielder
Date/Place of Birth: 17 June 1990 – Sunderland
England Debut: 17 November 2010 v France (H)

Since making his England debut back in 2010, Jordan has won over 80 international caps, twice been named England Player of the Year and has been included in the squad for six major international tournaments. His most recent inclusion in a Three Lions tournament squad came at the 2022 FIFA World Cup. He scored his third England goal at those finals in a 3-0 victory over Senegal in the round of 16.

DECLAN RICE

Legacy Number: 1241
Position: Midfielder
Date/Place of Birth: 14 January 1999 – London
England Debut: 22 March 2019 v Czech Republic (H)

After a successful debut season at Arsenal, Declan was included in England's squad for Euro 2024 – his third major international tournament having also featured at Euro 2020 and the 2022 FIFA World Cup. The midfielder appeared in all seven of England's matches at Euro 2024, where he achieved a passing accuracy of 91.29, completing 490 of his 530 passes. He made 46 ball recoveries – more than any other player at the tournament - and also made one assist and hit the opposition woodwork during his time in Germany.

KALVIN PHILLIPS

Legacy Number: 1250
Position: Midfielder
Date/Place of Birth: 2 December 1995 – Leeds
England Debut: 8 September 2020 v Denmark (A)

Kalvin's most recent international appearance at the time of writing had come against North Macedonia in November 2023, which brought his senior caps tally to 31. The midfielder started all seven UEFA Euro 2020 matches which led to him being named England Men's Player of the Year for 2020-21. His first international goal came in a 7-0 win against North Macedonia in a Euro 2024 qualifier in June 2023.

CONOR GALLAGHER

Legacy Number: 1266   Position: Midfielder
Date/Place of Birth: 6 February 2000 – Epsom
England Debut: 15 November 2021 v San Marino (A)

Conor made one start and four substitute appearances at Euro 2024, playing a total of 118 minutes. During that time, he covered an impressive 16.24km, as he made one block, three ball recoveries and completed 46 passes. In his first 18 England appearances, which began with the 10-0 win in San Marino in November 2021, Conor was only on the losing team on two occasions while the Three Lions triumphed in 13 of those games.

ADAM WHARTON

Legacy Number: 1282   Position: Midfielder
Date/Place of Birth: 6 February 2004 – Blackburn
England Debut: 3 June 2024 v Bosnia and Herzegovina (H)

Adam became the 1282nd and most recent men's player to play for England at the time of writing when he came on as a 62nd-minute substitute for Kieran Trippier in the 3-0 friendly win over Bosnia and Herzegovina in June 2024. He was named in Gareth Southgate's 26-player squad for Euro 2024, joining Crystal Palace teammates Dean Henderson, Marc Guéhi and Eberechi Eze in Germany.

KOBBIE MAINOO

Legacy Number: 1280   Position: Midfielder
Date/Place of Birth: 19 April 2005 – Stockport
England Debut: 23 March 2024 v Brazil (H)

Kobbie made nine appearances in his debut season as a senior England international, during which time he featured in six matches at Euro 2024. During his 370 minutes of football at the tournament, the midfielder boasted an impressive 92.5 passing accuracy, completing 190 of his 206 attempted passes. Prior to Euro 2024, Kobbie was just 18 years, 11 months and 4 days old when he made his debut in the 1-0 defeat to Brazil at Wembley Stadium in March 2024.

OLLIE WATKINS

Legacy Number: 1259   Position: Forward
Date/Place of Birth: 30 December 1995 – Torquay
England Debut: 25 March 2021 v San Marino (H)

Taking one touch to control the ball, before turning and striking it with his second, Ollie's last-minute winner against the Netherlands in the Euro 2024 semi-final is a goal we'll be seeing replays of for decades to come! Ollie's fourth senior international goal on the advent of his 14th cap came during a tournament in which he made three substitute appearances.

JUDE BELLINGHAM

Legacy Number: 1258 Position: Forward

Date/Place of Birth: 29 June 2003 – Stourbridge

England Debut: 12 November 2020 v Republic of Ireland (H)

Jude's stoppage-time overhead kick and subsequent outstretched arms celebration after scoring in the 2-1 extra-time win over Slovakia in the round of 16 is one of the iconic moments of England's memorable Euro 2024 campaign. Hot on the heels of winning both La Liga and the UEFA Champions League in his debut season with Real Madrid in 2023-24, Jude shone at the European Championships. In addition to his goal against Slovakia, he also scored a group stage winner against Serbia as he appeared in all seven tournament matches.

EBERECHI EZE

Legacy Number: 1273 Position: Forward

Date/Place of Birth: 29 June 1998 – London

England Debut: 16 June 2023 v Malta (A)

Eberechi appeared three times as a substitute at Euro 2024. One of four Crystal Palace players in Gareth Southgate's squad for the tournament, the winger played a pass to Ivan Toney, who crossed the ball into the box for Harry Kane's winner in the 2-1 extra-time triumph over Slovakia in the round of 16.

HARRY KANE

Legacy Number: 1207 Position: Forward

Date/Place of Birth: 28 July 1993 – London

England Debut: 27 March 2015 v Lithuania (H)

England's record goalscorer, Harry's three strikes at Euro 2024 saw him finish as the tournament's leading marksman along with five other players. Those goals took his overall international goal tally to 66 in 98 matches. Transferred to Bayern Munich in the summer of 2023, the Three Lions skipper won the European Golden Shoe award in his debut season at the Allianz Arena as he netted 36 times in the Bundesliga. He previously won the Golden Boot at the 2018 FIFA World Cup with six strikes in as many games and, during his time with Tottenham Hotspur, he became Premier League's second highest all-time goalscorer after Alan Shearer with 213 goals.

JARROD BOWEN

Legacy Number: 1271 Position: Forward

Date/Place of Birth: 20 December 1996 – Leominster

England Debut: 26 March 2023 v Hungary (A)

Jarrod made substitute appearances in England's first two group fixtures at Euro 2024 against Serbia and Denmark – the latter of which marked his 10th senior international cap. The scorer of West Ham United's winning goal in the 2023 UEFA Europa Conference League Final against Fiorentina, the forward played a total of six matches for the Three Lions in 2023-24.

JACK GREALISH

Legacy Number: 1251   Position: Forward
Date/Place of Birth: 10 September 1995 – Birmingham
England Debut: 8 September 2020 v Denmark (A)

Despite missing out on a place in Gareth Southgate's squad for Euro 2024, the 2023-24 season was a hugely successful one for Jack, as he won his third consecutive Premier League title with Manchester City. The midfielder has won over 30 caps for his country to date and made five appearances at both Euro 2020 and the 2022 World Cup. He made two assists at Euro 2020, setting up Raheem Sterling's winner against Czechia and Harry Kane's goal in the 2-0 round of 16 triumph over Germany.

PHIL FODEN

Legacy Number: 1247   Position: Forward
Date/Place of Birth: 28 May 2000 – Stockport
England Debut: 5 September 2020 v Iceland (A)

Phil appeared in all seven of England's matches at Euro 2024, completing 314 passes in the 622 minutes of football he played. He displayed his attacking instincts during the tournament with 13 dribbles and 12 runs into key play areas. Phil made his mark at previous tournaments too, with three appearances at Euro 2020, while he scored in the 3-0 win over Wales at the 2022 World Cup – one of four appearances at those finals in Qatar.

BUKAYO SAKA

Legacy Number: 1253   Position: Forward
Date/Place of Birth: 5 September 2001 – London
England Debut: 8 October 2020 v Wales (H)

Bukayo provided a moment of magic at Euro 2024 as his curling, left-footed effort from the edge of the penalty area drew England level in their quarter-final meeting with Switzerland and they went on to win on penalties. Fittingly, Bukayo was one of England's five scorers in the resulting shootout after the game finished 1-1 after extra-time. Arguably the Three Lions' most influential player at the tournament, Saka supplied the cross for Jude Bellingham's header against Serbia in the 1-0 Group C victory while he made 26 dribbles and 18 runs into key play areas in his 635 minutes of football in Germany.

ANTHONY GORDON

Legacy Number:1278   Position: Forward
Date/Place of Birth: 24 February 2001 – Liverpool
England Debut: 23 March 2024 v Brazil (H)

Anthony's debut season for England's senior team saw him make four appearances, including his tournament bow against Slovenia at Euro 2024. Previously capped between U16 and U21 level, the forward was named Player of the Tournament as England won the 2023 UEFA European Under-21 Championships in Georgia/Romania. He scored twice in the competition – in the 2-0 group stage victory over Israel and 1-0 quarter-final triumph against Portugal.

MARCUS RASHFORD

Legacy Number: 1215   Position: Forward
Date/Place of Birth: 31 October 1997 – Manchester
England Debut: 27 May 2016 v Australia (H)

Marcus made seven England appearances during the 2023-24 season, with his strike against Italy in October 2023 helping the Three Lions to a 3-1 victory and eventual qualification for Euro 2024. The forward came on as a substitute in the 1-0 defeat to Brazil at Wembley in March 2024, which marked his 60th senior international appearance. He had scored 17 England goals by that point in his career.

JAMES MADDISON

Legacy Number: 1245   Position: Forward
Date/Place of Birth: 23 November 1996 – Coventry
England Debut: 14 November 2019 v Montenegro (H)

Moving from Leicester City to Tottenham Hotspur in the summer of 2023, James made an instant impression in N17 with three goals in his first nine Premier League matches. The forward made four England appearances during the 2023-24 season but his progress was halted midway through the campaign as an injury sustained in a match against Chelsea saw him ruled out for the best part of three months.

CALLUM WILSON

Legacy Number: 1239   Position: Forward
Date/Place of Birth: 27 February 1992 – Coventry
England Debut: 15 November 2018 v United States (H)

Callum appeared in two qualifying matches on England's journey to Euro 2024, netting in the 4-0 win in Malta in June 2023. His one and only appearance for the Three Lions during the 2023-24 season came in the 3-1 win over Scotland at Hampden Park in September 2023, in which he came on as an 84th-minute substitute for Harry Kane.

IVAN TONEY

Legacy Number: 1272   Position: Forward
Date/Place of Birth: 16 March 1996 – Northampton
England Debut:26 March 2023 v Ukraine (H)

Ivan was coolness personified as he struck home one of England's five successful penalties in the quarter-final victory over Switzerland at Euro 2024 without even looking at the ball! The forward took social media by storm with a subsequent video that saw him bring his no-look penalty approach to winning at Connect Four, scoring a basket and bullseye. Aside from the match against Switzerland, Ivan made two other substitute appearances for England at Euro 2024.

Name: Sarina Wiegman
Date of Birth: 26 October 1969
Place of Birth: The Hague, Netherlands

Sarina Wiegman has overseen the greatest period in the history of England Women's football. UEFA EURO 2022 Champions, Women's Finalissima winners, back-to-back Arnold Clark Cup victors, World Cup runners-up… and the Dutchwoman and her Lionesses will be heading to Switzerland in the summer of 2025 to defend their European title.

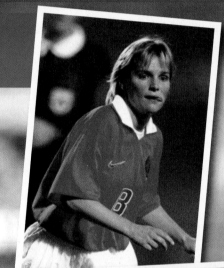

It's been quite a ride since Sarina took the reins of the England women's national team in September 2021. Just 10 months later her team won every match at UEFA Women's EURO 2022 - scoring an impressive 22 goals in the process - to lift their first-ever major trophy.

Not only was it historic for the Lionesses, but also for Wiegman as she became the first coach to win back-to-back tournaments having led her native Netherlands to the Women's EURO 2017 title five years earlier.

There were accolades for her players, and many for Sarina herself too. She won the UEFA Women's Coach of the Year Award in both 2021-22 and 2022-23 and the Best FIFA Women's Coach three times. She was awarded with a CBE for her services to association football in 2022.

In her playing days as a midfielder, Wiegman gained 104 caps for her country, becoming the first female player to reach a century of appearances and she captained the national side during an impressive career.

And after moving into coaching, she's remained a trailblazer in her homeland and become one of the big names in the women's game.

After starting out coaching with girls' grassroots teams in her local region of the Hague once her career on the pitch came to an end, her club coaching career began with a season-long spell with her former club Ter Leede

whom she led to the title and KNVB Cup in 2007. Sarina's first move into full-time coaching came soon after when she took over at ADO Den Haag in the newly formed Women's Eredivisie.

Wiegman quickly caught the eye too, by building a team and culture which would lead to them winning a league and cup double in 2012 before retaining the Cup in the following season. This didn't go unnoticed by the KNVB, and she was snapped up to be the assistant coach with the national team in 2014, working under Roger Reijners and then Arjan van der Laan.

In 2016, alongside her role with the national side Sarina was appointed assistant manager of the Sparta Rotterdam men's youth team which saw her become the first woman to coach in the professional men's game in the Netherlands.

After two spells as caretaker coach of the national team following the departures of Reijners and Van der Laan, she was finally granted the head coach role on a permanent basis in January 2017 – the start of an extraordinary year which would see her profile catapulted into another dimension both at home and abroad.

WOMEN'S SENIOR TEAM

PLAYER PROFILES

MARY EARPS

Legacy Number: 198 Position: Goalkeeper
Date of Birth: 7 March 1993 Place of Birth: Nottingham
England Debut: 11 June 2017 v Switzerland (A)

Mary's outstanding performances between the sticks have earned her a number of accolades in recent years. Just months after being awarded the Golden Glove for keeping three clean sheets as England reached the final of the 2023 FIFA Women's World Cup, the shot stopper came fifth in the Ballon d'Or Féminin (the highest a goalkeeper has placed), was voted the BBC Sports Personality of the Year for 2023, received an MBE in the 2024 New Year Honours and was named The Best FIFA Women's Goalkeeper for a second successive year. Mary - who signed for Paris Saint-Germain in the summer of 2024 - also played a key role in the Lionesses' famous triumph at UEFA Women's EURO 2022, keeping four clean sheets in six matches.

HANNAH HAMPTON

Legacy Number: 222 Position: Goalkeeper
Date of Birth: 16 November 2000 Place of Birth: Birmingham
England Debut: 20 February 2022 v Spain (N*)
*Neutral venue for the Arnold Clark Cup but played on home soil at Norwich City FC's Carrow Road.

Hannah kept a clean sheet in her first start of England's UEFA Women's EURO 2025 qualifying campaign - a 2-0 win over the Republic of Ireland in April 2024 while she came on as a substitute for the injured Mary Earps in the 2-1 defeat to France in Newcastle one month later. Whilst winning her sixth cap against France on 4 June 2024, she made a match-winning save in the 89th minute of the EURO qualifier to help England secure an important three points. A member of the Lionesses squad for both UEFA Women's EURO 2022 and the 2023 FIFA Women's World Cup, Hannah won the Barclays Women's Super League with Chelsea in 2023-24 after signing for the London club in the summer of 2023.

KHIARA KEATING

Legacy Number: N/A Position: Goalkeeper
Date of Birth: 27 June 2004 Place of Birth: Manchester
England Debut: Yet to make senior debut at the time of writing

After an impressive start to the 2023-24 Barclays Women's Super League season with Manchester City, Khiara received her first senior England call-up against Belgium in the UEFA Women's Nations League in October 2023. Though she didn't feature for the Lionesses on that occasion, the young goalkeeper has represented England between WU15 and WU19 levels and has been named in the WU23 squad twice.

LUCY THOMAS

Legacy Number: N/A **Position:** Goalkeeper
Date of Birth: 21 March 2000 **Place of Birth:** Farnborough
England Debut: Yet to make senior debut at the time of writing

Lucy first featured in the England senior squad as a standby player for the UEFA Women's EURO 2025 qualifying games in the summer of 2024, before an injury to Mary Earps saw her named on the bench for their victory over France on 4 June 2024. A regular for the Young Lionesses at development level, Lucy's call up came after an impressive season for Birmingham City in the Barclays Women's Championship as well as in the WU23s.

ANNA MOORHOUSE

Legacy Number: N/A **Position:** Goalkeeper
Date of Birth: 30 March 1995 **Place of Birth:** Oldham
England Debut: Yet to make senior debut at the time of writing

Anna was called up to the senior squad by Sarina Wiegman for England's final two UEFA Women's EURO 2025 qualifiers against the Republic of Ireland and Sweden in July 2024. Following spells with Barclays Women's Super League sides Arsenal and West Ham United, the goalkeeper has spent the last four years playing club football overseas for Bordeaux in France and her current club Orlando Pride in the United States.

KAYLA RENDELL

Legacy Number: N/A **Position:** Goalkeeper
Date of Birth: 29 June 2001 **Place of Birth:** Poole
England Debut: Yet to make senior debut at the time of writing

A regular for the England WU23s, Kayla received her first call-up to the senior squad in April 2024 for the UEFA Women's EURO 25 qualifiers against Sweden and the Republic of Ireland. First choice goalkeeper for Barclays Women's Championship side Southampton, where she was voted Player of the Season for 2022-23, Kayla has also represented her country between WU16 and WU21 levels.

MILLIE BRIGHT

Legacy Number: 197 **Position:** Defender
Date of Birth: 21 August 1993 **Place of Birth:** Chesterfield
England Debut: 20 September 2016 v Belgium (A)

One of the most experienced members of the Lionesses squad, Millie won her 81st cap in their 0-0 draw with Sweden in the UEFA Women's EURO 2025 qualifying fixture in July 2024. She skippered her country to the final of the 2023 FIFA Women's World Cup and, along with Mary Earps and Alex Greenwood, played every minute of the tournament. A reliable presence at the back, Millie was also a key figure for England at UEFA Women's EURO 2022 when they lifted the trophy. The centre-back - who won the Barclays Women's Super League with Chelsea in 2023-24 - was awarded an OBE in the 2024 New Year Honours list.

LUCY BRONZE

Legacy Number: 181 Position: Defender
Date of Birth: 28 October 1991 Place of Birth: Berwick-upon-Tweed
England Debut: 26 June 2013 v Japan (H)

Lucy has been one of England's most consistent and impressive players for more than a decade and has 125 caps at the time of writing. She finished as runner-up in the Ballon d'Or Féminin in 2019 and a year later became the first English player to claim The Best FIFA Women's Player award. Lucy has won every domestic honour in England and, with Barcelona, she collected Liga F and UEFA Women's Champions League winners' medals in 2023-24. The right-back has been included in Lionesses squads for six major tournaments to date – including their triumph at UEFA Women's EURO 2022 – and featured in five of England's qualifying games for the UEFA Women's EURO 2025 in Switzerland.

JESS CARTER

Legacy Number: 201 Position: Defender
Date of Birth: 27 October 1997 Place of Birth: Warwick
England Debut: 28 November 2017 v Kazakhstan (H)

Jess featured in all six of England's UEFA Women's EURO 2025 qualifying matches, bringing her caps tally to 36. The versatile player has become a regular under Sarina Wiegman and appeared in six of their seven 2023 FIFA Women's World Cup games, including the final against Spain. The defender scored her first international goal in England's record-breaking 20-0 defeat of Latvia in November 2021, while she netted her second in a 7-1 friendly triumph over Austria in February 2024.

ALEX GREENWOOD

Legacy Number: 184 Position: Defender
Date of Birth: 7 September 1993 Place of Birth: Liverpool
England Debut: 5 March 2014 v Italy (N)

Set-piece specialist Alex scored England's second goal from the penalty spot as they beat the Republic of Ireland 2-0 in a UEFA Women's EURO 2025 qualifier on 9 April 2024. That appearance was her 92nd for the Lionesses, and she has netted seven international goals at the time of writing. The Manchester City defender was ever-present during England's seven matches at the 2023 FIFA Women's World Cup and she also appeared in five of the Lionesses' six games en route to European Championship glory in July 2022.

NIAMH CHARLES

Legacy Number: 220 Position: Defender
Date of Birth: 21 June 1999 Place of Birth: Wirral
England Debut: 9 April 2021 v France (A)

Niamh won her 18th cap in England's 0-0 draw with Sweden in July 2024 during their UEFA Women's EURO qualifying campaign. The defender also started their friendly matches against Italy and Austria in February 2024, on the back of two substitute appearances for the Lionesses at the 2023 FIFA Women's World Cup. She was part of Sarina Wiegman's squad who won the Arnold Clark Cup in 2022 and 2023, and at club level won the Barclays Women's Super League with Chelsea in 2023-24.

ESME MORGAN

Legacy Number: 224 Position: Defender
Date of Birth: 18 October 2000 Place of Birth: Sheffield
England Debut: 12 October 2022 v Czech Republic (H)

A regular across development age groups, Esme made her senior England debut against the Czech Republic in October 2022. Since then, she has won a further seven caps, including starting in the Lionesses' 7-2 triumph over Austria in a friendly in February 2024. The centre-back, who signed for the National Women's Soccer League side Washington Spirit in June 2024, was included in the Lionesses squad for the 2023 FIFA Women's World Cup.

LOTTE WUBBEN-MOY

Legacy Number: 217 Position: Defender
Date of Birth: 11 January 1999 Place of Birth: London
England Debut: 23 February 2021 v Northern Ireland (H)

Lotte scored her first Lionesses goal in their 5-1 friendly victory over Italy in February 2024 before picking up her 13th England cap in their 1-1 draw with Sweden to open their UEFA Women's EURO 2025 qualifying campaign. The Arsenal defender was an unused substitute for England's victory over Brazil in the inaugural Women's Finalissima and she was also included in the Lionesses squad for the UEFA European Women's Championship in 2022 and the 2023 FIFA Women's World Cup. Following an excellent campaign for the Gunners in 2023-24, Lotte was named their Player of the Season.

LEAH WILLIAMSON

Legacy Number: 205 Position: Defender/Midfielder
Date of Birth: 29 March 1997 Place of Birth: Milton Keynes
England Debut: 8 June 2018 v Russia (A)

Just three months after being given the England captaincy, Leah wrote her name in the history books when she became the first woman to lift a major trophy with England, as they beat Germany in the UEFA Women's EURO 2022 Final at Wembley Stadium connected by EE. She went on to lead the team to success over Brazil at the Women's Finalissima in 2023 but a knee injury ruled her out of the summer's FIFA Women's World Cup in Australia. The skipper returned to the England camp for their UEFA Women's EURO 2025 qualifying campaign, winning her 48th cap in their 0-0 draw with Sweden on 16 July 2024.

MAYA LE TISSIER

Legacy Number: 226 Position: Defender
Date of Birth: 18 April 2002 Place of Birth: Guernsey
England Debut: 15 November 2022 v Norway (N)

Maya made her senior England debut on 15 November 2022, as she played all 90 minutes of a 1-1 draw with Norway. Her call-up came after an impressive start to the 2022-23 season with Manchester United, whom she had joined that summer. Maya had previously captained England's WU15s and WU17s, and featured for her country at WU19 and WU23 level before making the step up to the senior squad. She won her fourth England cap for the Lionesses during a 2-1 victory over the Republic of Ireland in a UEFA Women's EURO 2025 qualifier on 12 July 2024.

MILLIE TURNER

Legacy Number: 229 Position: Defender
Date of Birth: 7 July 1996 Place of Birth: Wilmslow
England Debut: 27 February 2024 v Italy (N)

Having been capped by England at WU19 and WU23 levels, Millie made the step up to the senior squad in September 2020 when she joined a training camp at St. George's Park. She was an unused substitute for two UEFA Women's Nations League matches in November 2023 before finally making her debut as a second-half substitute in a 5-1 friendly victory over Italy in February 2024. The defender was also included in the squad for the UEFA Women's EURO 2025 qualifying campaign. At club level, Millie had made 144 appearances for Manchester United as of the end of the 2023-24 season.

GEORGIA STANWAY

Legacy Number: 209 Position: Midfielder
Date of Birth: 3 January 1999 Place of Birth: Barrow-in-Furness
England Debut: 8 November 2018 v Austria (A)

Georgia scored from the penalty spot in England's much-needed 2-1 victory over the Republic of Ireland in July 2024 en route to qualification for UEFA Women's EURO 2025 in Switzerland. It was her 19th international goal in 71 appearances, since making her senior Lionesses debut against Austria in November 2018. A key player for Sarina Wiegman, she was one of the stars in their triumphant UEFA Women's EURO 2022 success, and helped her side reach the final of the 2023 FIFA Women's World Cup, converting a penalty to a give England a 1-0 victory over Haiti in their opening match. Georgia won the Frauen-Bundesliga with Bayern Munich in 2023-24 and was named the International Player of the Year at the 2024 Women's Football Awards.

ELLA TOONE

Legacy Number: 216 Position: Midfielder
Date of Birth: 2 September 1999 Place of Birth: Tyldesley
England Debut: 23 February 2021 v Northern Ireland (H)

A regular name on the England team sheet since Sarina Wiegman's arrival, Ella featured in five of the Lionesses' qualifying games for UEFA Women's EURO 2025 to bring her caps tally to 51. The attack-minded midfielder has scored some important goals for England, including against Brazil in the inaugural Women's Finalissima and in their 3-1 semi-final victory over Australia at the 2023 FIFA Women's World Cup. Ella, who won the Adobe Women's FA Cup with Manchester United in 2024, also scored twice during the UEFA European Women's Championship in 2022 which the Lionesses went on to win.

KEIRA WALSH

Legacy Number: 200 Position: Midfielder
Date of Birth: 8 April 1997 Place of Birth: Rochdale
England Debut: 28 November 2017 v Kazakhstan (H)

Being handed the captain's armband for England's opening game of their UEFA Women's EURO 2025 qualifying campaign is testament to Keira's vital role in the Lionesses' midfield. She dictates the play and leads by example. In the UEFA Women's EURO 2022 Final against Germany, she set up Ella Toone's opening goal and was named Player of the Match. At the following year's FIFA Women's World Cup, Keira featured in six out of England's seven matches as they reached the final. She won the quadruple with Barcelona in 2023-24 including the UEFA Women's Champions league and Liga F.

FRAN KIRBY

Legacy Number: 186 **Position:** Midfielder
Date of Birth: 29 June 1993 **Place of Birth:** Reading
England Debut: 3 August 2014 v Sweden (H)

Experienced midfielder Fran featured in four of England's six qualifying games for UEFA Women's EURO 2025 as she brought her senior caps tally to 73. She missed the 2023 FIFA Women's World Cup through injury but started in all six games for England during the UEFA Women's EURO in 2022, scoring in the group stage victory over Northern Ireland and the semi-final triumph against Sweden. At the time of writing, Fran has netted 19 times for the Lionesses since her debut in 2014. At club level, after playing almost 200 games for Chelsea and scoring 108 goals, she signed for Brighton & Hove Albion in the summer of 2024.

JESS PARK

Legacy Number:: 225 **Position:** Midfielder
Date of Birth: 21 October 2001 **Place of Birth:** Brough
England Debut: 11 November 2022 v Japan (N)

Jess scored 79 seconds into her senior England debut after coming off the bench in the 89th minute of a 4-0 victory over Japan in a friendly in November 2022. The Manchester City midfielder has made a further eight appearances for the Lionesses since then, with her first start coming in the 2023 Arnold Clark Cup against Italy. In September 2023, she was named in Sarina Wiegman's squad for the 2023-24 UEFA Nations League matches and started for the Lionesses in their UEFA Women's EURO 2025 qualifying triumphs over the Republic of Ireland in April and July 2024.

GRACE CLINTON

Legacy Number: 228 **Position:** Midfielder
Date of Birth: 31 March 2003 **Place of Birth:** Liverpool
England Debut: 23 February 2024 v Austria (N)

Grace netted within 20 minutes of her senior international debut in a 7–2 win over Austria in a friendly in February 2024. She caught Sarina Wiegman's eye while on loan with Tottenham Hotspur from Manchester United in 2023-24 while she has also played for Everton and Bristol City (loan) at club level. Grace started the Lionesses' opening UEFA Women's EURO 2025 qualifier against Sweden which finished 1-1, and was previously a regular for the Young Lionesses at a variety of levels between WU17 and WU23.

MISSY-BO KEARNS

Legacy Number: N/A **Position:** Midfielder
Date of Birth: 14 April 2001 **Place of Birth:** Liverpool
England Debut: Yet to make senior debut at the time of writing

Missy-Bo regularly represented England at WU17 and WU19 level before stepping up to the WU23s, whom she has gone on to captain. Following an impressive 2023-24 campaign for the Young Lionesses, the Liverpool player was rewarded with a first England senior call-up in May 2024 when she was named as part of the squad for four UEFA Women's EURO 2025 qualifying games as a standby player. In 2023, Missy-Bo won the Young Player of the Year prize at the Women's Football Awards.

KATIE ZELEM

Legacy Number: 221 Position: Midfielder
Date of Birth: 20 January 1996 Place of Birth: Oldham
England Debut: 30 November 2021 v Latvia (H)

Katie made her senior international debut in a significant match – England Women's record 20-0 victory over Latvia in November 2021. Capped between WU15 and WU23 level, Katie helped the WU19s to a second-place finish at the UEFA Women's U19 Euro finals in 2013 and represented England at the FIFA U20 World Cup in Canada a year later. She made two appearances at the 2023 FIFA Women's World Cup, as a starter against China and from the bench against Nigeria.

LAUREN HEMP

Legacy Number: 214 Position: Forward
Date of Birth: 7 August 2000 Place of Birth: North Walsham
England Debut: 8 October 2019 v Portugal (A)

The forward, who was awarded an MBE in January 2024, struck home three times in seven appearances at the 2023 FIFA Women's World Cup as the Lionesses reached the final. A year earlier, Lauren started every game as England triumphed at the UEFA Women's EURO 2022 Championship. She also featured in all of England's UEFA Women's EURO 2025 qualifying matches, with her direct running, skill, pace and threat in front of goal, making her one of Sarina Wiegman's star players.

CHLOE KELLY

Legacy Number: 212 Position: Forward
Date of Birth: 15 January 1998 Place of Birth: London
England Debut: 8 November 2018 v Austria (A)

Chloe's dramatic extra-time winner for the Lionesses in the UEFA Women's EURO 2022 Final against Germany sealed her place in English football history. The forward had played an important role from the bench throughout the tournament and did the same at the following year's FIFA Women's World Cup, scoring in England's 6–1 defeat over China and netting the winning penalty in the round of 16 shootout against Nigeria. Chloe came on as a substitute in all six UEFA Women's EURO 2025 qualifying matches too, bringing her caps tally to 45.

BETH MEAD

Legacy Number: 204 Position: Forward
Date of Birth: 9 May 1995 Place of Birth: Whitby
England Debut: 6 April 2018 v Wales (H)

Beth's goal in England's 2-1 defeat to France during the UEFA Women's EURO 2025 qualifier on 31 May 2024, brought her tally up to 33 in total. The goal-machine missed out on the 2023 FIFA Women's World Cup with injury but the previous year she picked up the Golden Boot and Player of the Tournament awards at the UEFA Women's EURO in 2022, having netted six times en route to the Lionesses' triumph on home soil. Her impressive performances also saw her collect a number of accolades in 2022 as she was named player of the year by England, the BBC and UEFA, while she also came runner-up in the Ballon d'Or Féminin and won BBC Sports Personality of the Year.

ALESSIA RUSSO

Legacy Number: 215 **Position:** Forward
Date of Birth: 8 February 1999 **Place of Birth:** Maidstone
England Debut: 11 March 2020 v Spain (N)

Alessia has netted some important goals for England in recent years. At the 2023 FIFA Women's World Cup, she scored the winner in a 2-1 quarter-final victory over Colombia before getting the Lionesses' third goal in the 3-1 triumph over Australia in the semi-final. The previous year, her audacious back-heel in England's semi-final victory over Sweden at the UEFA Women's EURO in 2022 earned the striker the Goal of the Tournament award. And on 12 July 2024, the Arsenal star scored her 20th international goal in just 41 games, when she netted England's opener against the Republic of Ireland in a UEFA Women's EURO 2025 qualifier to help her team secure a vital three points.

LAUREN JAMES

Legacy Number: 223 **Position:** Forward
Date of Birth: 29 September 2001 **Place of Birth:** London
England Debut: 3 September 2022 v Austria (A)

Chelsea's Player of the Season in 2023-24, Lauren started and scored in England's 2-0 victory over the Republic of Ireland in a UEFA Women's EURO 2025 qualifying game in April 2024. At the previous year's FIFA World Cup, Lauren played a key role in the Lionesses' run to the final with three strikes and three assists. Since making her debut in September 2022, Lauren has won 24 senior caps and netted seven goals at the time of writing.

AGGIE BEEVER-JONES

Legacy Number: 231 **Position:** Forward
Date of Birth: 27 July 2003 **Place of Birth:** London
England Debut: 12 July 2024 v Republic of Ireland (H)

Aggie made her senior England debut as an 89th-minute substitute in their 2-1 victory over the Republic of Ireland in the UEFA Women's EURO 2025 qualifier on 12 July 2024. After featuring for England at various youth levels from WU15 to WU23, her call-up to the senior squad came after an impressive season with Chelsea in the Barclays Women's Super League in 2023-24.

JESSICA NAZ

Legacy Number: 230 **Position:** Forward
Date of Birth: 24 September 2000 **Place of Birth:** London
England Debut: 12 July 2024 v Republic of Ireland (H)

Jess made her first senior Lionesses appearance when she came off the bench in the 71st minute of their victory over the Republic of Ireland during a UEFA Women's EURO 2025 qualifier in July 2024. The forward – who reached the final of the Adobe Women's FA Cup with Tottenham Hotspur in 2024 - has previously represented her country between WU17 and WU23 levels, and in October 2023 she scored the opener in a 2-0 win against Portugal in the U23 European League.

UEFA WOMEN'S EURO 2025 QUALIFIERS

Throughout the spring and summer of 2024, the Lionesses led a successful campaign to qualify for the 2025 Women's European Championships, to be staged in Switzerland in July 2025.

ENGLAND 1-1 SWEDEN
UEFA Women's Euro 2025 Qualifying – Group A3
5 April 2024 - Wembley Stadium, London

Defending Champions England drew 1-1 with Sweden in their opening Euro 2025 qualifier at Wembley Stadium. The Swedes made a bright start but it was the Lionesses who broke the deadlock on 24 minutes when Alessia Russo headed home Lauren James' cross. Georgia Stanway had a chance to make it two soon after but her long-range shot went wide.

Sweden equalised through a Fridolina Rolfö header midway through the second half and though England pushed for a winner, they couldn't find a way through a resolute Swedish defence and had to settle for a share of the spoils.

ENGLAND: Earps, Bronze, Charles (Carter 79), Walsh, Wubben-Moy, Greenwood, James (Mead 67), Stanway, Russo (Kelly 79), Clinton (Toone 57), Hemp

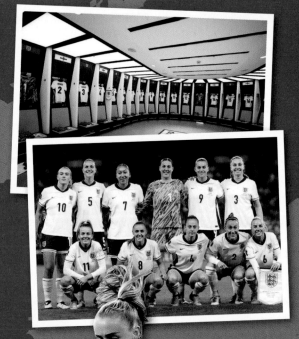

REPUBLIC OF IRELAND 0-2 ENGLAND

UEFA Women's Euro 2025 Qualifying – Group A3
9 April 2024 - Aviva Stadium, Dublin

First-half goals from Lauren James and Alex Greenwood saw the Lionesses record a 2-0 win over the Republic of Ireland in Dublin. Kiera Walsh's cross fell to James in the box and she slotted home on the 12-minute mark to open the scoring before Greenwood converted from the penalty spot six minutes later, after Ruesha Littlejohn handballed in the area.

Greenwood could have doubled her goal tally from the spot after half an hour following another handball, but this time she was denied by the post. Sarina Wiegman's side soaked up second-half pressure from the hosts and saw the game out for all three points.

ENGLAND: Hampton, Bronze, Carter, Walsh, Williamson, Greenwood, James (Kelly 86), Park (Kirby 56), Russo (Daly 86), Toone (Stanway 75), Hemp (Mead 56)

ENGLAND 1-2 FRANCE

UEFA Women's Euro 2025 Qualifying – Group A3
31 May 2024 - St. James' Park, Newcastle

Beth Mead netted her 33rd international goal to give England the lead after half an hour of their clash with France. The Lionesses had suffered an early blow after losing goalkeeper Mary Earps to injury in the opening minutes, but they rallied to go in front. The visitors fought back and equalised just before the break through Élisa De Almeida and with 20 minutes of the match in Newcastle remaining, Marie-Antoinette Katoto hit a strike to give France the victory.

ENGLAND: Earps (Hampton 8), Bronze, Carter, Walsh, Bright, Williamson, Mead (Kelly 79), Stanway (Kirby 79), Russo, Toone, Hemp

FRANCE 1-2 ENGLAND
UEFA Women's Euro 2025 Qualifying – Group A3
4 June 2024 - Stade Geoffroy-Guichard, Saint-Étienne

Just four days after their defeat to France in Newcastle, Sarina Wiegman's side travelled to Saint-Étienne looking for revenge against the same opponents. And they got it. A 21st-minute Georgia Stanway strike put England 1-0 up and Alessia Russo doubled their advantage just after the half-hour mark.

France pulled one back from the penalty spot through Kadidiatou Diani, following a foul by Leah Williamson, but England refused to surrender their lead and they took maximum points.

ENGLAND: Hampton, Bronze, Carter, Walsh, Bright, Williamson, Mead (Kelly 75), Stanway, Russo, Toone (Kirby 90), Hemp

ENGLAND 2-1 REPUBLIC OF IRELAND
UEFA Women's Euro 2025 Qualifying – Group A3
12 July 2024 - Carrow Road, Norwich

Alessia Russo and Georgia Stanway were on target for the Lionesses once again as they saw off the Republic of Ireland 2-1 in their penultimate Euro 2025 qualifier. Russo netted her third strike of the campaign after just five minutes at Norwich City's Carrow Road to give them a 1-0 lead at the break.

Then, when the referee pointed to the spot after Ireland's Niamh Fahey fouled Lauren Hemp in front of goal on 57 minutes, Stanway stepped up and coolly converted the resulting penalty. Julie-Ann Russell got a goal back for Ireland in the last minute of the match, but it proved a mere consolation.

ENGLAND: Hampton, Le Tissier, Williamson (Bright 46), Greenwood, Carter (Charles 46), Stanway, Walsh, Park, Hemp (Beever-Jones 89), Russo (Naz 71), Mead (Kelly 61)

SWEDEN 0-0 ENGLAND
UEFA Women's Euro 2025 Qualifying – Group A3
16 July 2024 - Gamla Ullevi, Gothenburg

The Lionesses booked their place at the 2025 Women's European Championships after picking up a point against Sweden. Both sides were looking to secure the remaining automatic qualification spot in Group A3 so it was a hard-fought game in Gothenburg.

England dominated possession in the first half but were unable to get past a strong Swedish defence. The hosts were livelier in the second period, knowing only a win would see them avoid the play-offs, and they piled on the pressure as the minutes ticked by. Sarina Wiegman's side stood firm though, and qualified in second place behind France.

ENGLAND: Hampton, Bronze, Williamson, Bright, Carter, Walsh, Stanway, Toone (Kirby 90+3), Hemp (Charles 90), Mead (Kelly 74), Russo

Final Group A3 Table

		P	W	D	L	GF	GA	GD	PTS
1	France (Q)	6	4	0	2	8	7	+1	12
2	England (Q)	6	3	2	1	8	5	+3	11
3	Sweden (Q)	6	2	2	2	6	4	+2	8
4	Republic of Ireland	6	1	0	5	4	10	-6	3

UEFA WOMEN'S EURO 2025

Inaugural Championships 1984

Reigning Champions England are one of 16 teams who will compete in the 14th edition of the UEFA Women's Championships, which will be hosted in Switzerland between 2 and 27 July 2025.

LOWDOWN

On 16 July 2024, England's goalless draw with Sweden in their final Group A3 game was enough to seal automatic qualification to UEFA Women's Euro 2025. The other automatic qualifiers to the tournament are Germany, Spain, Iceland, Denmark, France, Italy and the Netherlands along with hosts Switzerland. A play-off tournament was set to be played between 23 October and 3 December 2024 to determine the other seven teams to compete in the finals.

The draw for the finals was due to take place on 16 December 2024, with hosts Switzerland assigned position A1 in Group A. We have left space for you to fill in England's tournament fixtures, final group table and route to the final (hopefully!) overleaf!

REIGNING CHAMPIONS

Prior to 2025, England had competed in nine of the 13 previous editions of the Women's European Championships. They were runners-up in the inaugural Championships back in 1984 and once again in 2009 while they were also semi-finalists in 1995 and 2017.

On home soil in 2022, the Lionesses were finally victorious during a memorable summer. Sarina Wiegman's side began their road to glory by topping Group A with victories over Austria (1-0), Norway (8-0) and Northern Ireland (5-0).

Esther González put Spain 1-0 up in a keenly fought quarter-final at Brighton & Hove Albion's Falmer Stadium on 20 July 2022 but a late Ella Toone goal forced extra-time and Georgia Stanway won it for the Lionesses in the added period of 30 minutes.

England made light work of Sweden in their semi-final at Bramall Lane, Sheffield six days later. Beth Mead's first-half strike was added to in the second period by goals from Lucy Bronze, Alessia Russo - with an audacious backheel - and Fran Kirby.

Just after the hour mark, England took the lead in the final — played in front of a crowd of 87,192 at Wembley Stadium on 31 July 2022. Germany's Lina Magull levelled with 11 minutes on the clock, as a Lionesses match once again went into extra-time. With penalties looming, Chloe Kelly scored with 10 minutes remaining to secure victory. Kelly's goal, and subsequent celebration, instantly gained a place in English football history!

STADIUMS

UEFA Women's Euro 2025 kicks off on 2 July 2025 when hosts Switzerland play their first Group A match at the 38,512-capacity St. Jakob-Park, home of FC Basel. The same stadium will also host the final on 27 July 2025.

Seven other stadiums and cities will host tournament matches. The 30,084 Stade de Genève – which saw a memorable 3-2 win for England Men over Argentina in 2005 – will host three group games, a quarter-final and a semi-final match, as will the iconic Stadion Letzigrund in FC Zürich. Also an athletics venue, it was at the Letzigrund on 21 June 1960 that Armin Hary became the first person to run the 100 metres in 10.0 seconds.

The quarter-final stadium line-up is completed by the Stadion Wankdorf in Bern.

The other tournament venues are the Stockhorn Arena in Thun, the Stade de Tourbillon in Sion, St. Gallen's Kybunpark and the Swissporarena, Lucerne.

St. Jakob-Park

TOURNAMENT PLANNER Fill in the blanks

England are in Group ___ at UEFA Women's Euro 2025.
Fixture information can be found at www.uefa.com/womenseuro

GROUP ___ RESULTS

KNOCKOUT PHASE RESULTS (IF APPLICABLE)

GROUP MATCH 1	DATE:	JULY 2025
VENUE:		
SCORE: England		OPPONENT
ENGLAND SCORER(S)		

GROUP MATCH 2	DATE:	JULY 2025
VENUE:		
SCORE: England		OPPONENT
ENGLAND SCORER(S)		

GROUP MATCH 3	DATE:	JULY 2025
VENUE:		
SCORE: England		OPPONENT
ENGLAND SCORER(S)		

QUARTER-FINAL	DATE:	JULY 2025
VENUE:		
SCORE: England		OPPONENT
ENGLAND SCORER(S)		

SEMI-FINAL	DATE:	JULY 2025
VENUE:		
SCORE: England		OPPONENT
ENGLAND SCORER(S)		

FINAL	DATE: 27 JULY 2025
VENUE:	
SCORE: England	OPPONENT
ENGLAND SCORER(S)	

FINAL GROUP ___ STANDINGS
(TOP TWO TEAMS ADVANCE TO KNOCKOUT PHASE)

TOURNAMENT WINNER:

Pos	Team	Pld	W	D	L	GF	GA	GD	Pts

2023-24 IN REVIEW

A look back on the 2023-24 season for other England teams

WOMEN'S U23s

Led by head coach Emma Coates, the England women's under-23s team took part in a new, structured league competition during the 2023-24 campaign. The WU23s lined up alongside Belgium, France, Italy, Netherlands, Norway, Portugal, Spain and Sweden.

England drew 1-1 in Norway in their league opener on 21 September 2023. Aggie Beever-Jones was on target for Coates' side in Bryne. Beever-Jones also netted in a 3-0 win over Belgium in a match played at Shrewsbury Town's New Meadow Stadium four days later.

The WU23s' unbeaten run in the competition continued through until the end of the calendar year. Poppy Pattinson netted in a 1-1 away draw against Italy while

Jessica Naz and Kiera Skeels scored in a 2-0 triumph over Portugal at Manchester City's Academy Stadium. A Katie Robinson goal helped England to an impressive 1-0 win in France before a home clash with Spain at St. George's Park ended in a 1-1 draw.

Leading 1-0 against the Netherlands, through a Hannah Silcock goal, going into stoppage time at the end of the 90 minutes on 26 February 2024, the WU23s looked set for another three points, but Fenna Kalma levelled for the visitors with pretty much the last kick of the game at the Banús Football Centre in Marbella, Spain. AFC Telford's New Bucks Head ground staged a 3-1 England win over Sweden on 4 April 2024.

MEN'S U21s

Prior to an away game against Northern Ireland in September 2024 and home clashes against Ukraine and Azerbaijan a month later, England under-21s were in a commanding position in UEFA European Under-21 Qualification Group F, with six victories and just one defeat leaving them joint-top of the six-team group.

A 3-0 victory in Luxembourg on 11 September 2023 gave Lee Carsley's side a perfect start to qualifying and this was followed by a 9-1 thrashing of Serbia at Nottingham Forest's City Ground on 12 October 2023 – a match in which Jaden Philogene, Harvey Elliott and Noni Madueke all bagged braces.

After England's only defeat in the group at the time of writing – a 3-2 reverse against Ukraine in a match played in Košice, Slovakia – the Young Lions returned to winning ways with a 3-0 triumph in Serbia. James McAtee scored twice in that victory. The last fixture of the calendar year ended with a 3-0 win over Northern Ireland at Goodison Park on 21 November 2023 as Elliott scored another brace.

Elliott took his goal tally for the qualifying campaign to seven with a further double in a 5-1 win in Azerbaijan on 22 March 2024. A 7-0 thrashing of Luxembourg in Bolton four days later – a game that featured braces from Madueke, Samuel Iling-Junior and Morgan Rogers – left the Young Lions on the brink of qualification for UEFA Under-21 Euro 2025, which will be staged in Slovakia on 12-29 June 2025.

MEN'S U20s

England's under-20s experienced mixed results in the 2023/24 European Elite League. The Young Lions suffered three consecutive defeats to Romania (0-2), Portugal (1-2) and Italy (0-3) in their first three matches of the campaign. Twice coming from behind, a 3-2 victory in Germany on 20 November 2023 heralded a turnaround in fortunes for the side. Mateo Joseph, Samuel Edozie and Charlie Webster were the goalscorers in front of a crowd of 9,700 at the Jahnstadion Regensburg.

Dane Scarlett scored a hat-trick – which included a penalty – as England triumphed 5-1 in Poland on 22 March 2024. Tim Iroegbunam and Ben Nelson were also on target in the convincing win. And Scarlett netted twice more in a 3-1 win over Czechia on 26 March 2024 – a game in which Ollie Arblaster got his first MU23s goal.

MEN'S U19s

England's under-19s competed in two friendly matches in Morocco in March 2024. In the first of those fixtures, an own-goal just before half-time gave home side Morocco the lead at the Stade Moulay Hassan in Rabat before Chelsea defender Billy Gee equalised with ten minutes remaining. Three days later, the MU19s were defeated 3-2 by the USA at the Complexe Mohammed VI. The Young Lions' goals came from Bailey Cadamarteri and Leo Castledine.

MEN'S U18s

England's under-18s rounded off their 2023-24 season by winning the inaugural U18 Tri-Nations Trophy. They kicked off the tournament, staged at St. George's Park, with a 4-2 triumph over Northern Ireland. First-half goals from Kadan Young, Romelle Donovan and Ethan Wheatley helped seal the victory for Tom Curtis' side while Ajay Matthews' deflected effort rounded off the scoring. Four days later, a second-half brace from Wheatley saw England to a 2-1 win over Morocco and allowed captain Lewis Orford to lift the trophy.

WOMEN'S U19s

England women's under-19s played no less than 13 matches during the 2023-24 season. The campaign saw the WU19s successfully navigate qualification to the eight-team, 2024 UEFA Women's Under-19 Championship, which was staged in Lithuania between 14 and 27 July 2024.

In round one of the Euros qualification campaign, which was staged in South Wales in October 2023, England beat Greece (2-0) and Czechia (1-0) and also thrashed Wales 6-1 at Dragon Park in Newport to jump the first hurdle. After competing in the Algarve Cup in the winter of 2023 and playing friendlies against France and Norway in February 2024, interim head coach John Griffiths oversaw victories over Switzerland (2-0), Portugal (1-0) and Italy (4-1) in Portugal that allowed his side to progress to the 2024 UEFA Women's Under-19 Championship finals.

MEN'S U17s

England men's under-17s' run at the 2024 UEFA U17 Euros came to an agonising end at the quarter-final stage, falling to defeat in a penalty shootout against Italy after their match at the AEK Arena in Larnaca finished in a 1-1 draw.

Having beaten France (4-0) and Spain (3-1) in the group stage of the competition, Nathan Nwaneri put the MU17s 1-0 up against Italy after just 16 minutes of the last-eight clash on 30 May 2024. There were no further goals after Mattia Liberali levelled for the Azzurri. And it was Italy who went on to win the competition with a 3-0 triumph over Portugal in the final.

WOMEN'S U17s

Having reached the semi-finals of the UEFA Women's Under-17 Championship in 2023, England's under-17 women went one better in 2024 by finishing as tournament runners-up.

During a season in which the WU17s enjoyed a run of 13-straight wins across all competitions, Natalie Henderson's side got off to an excellent start to the 2024 UEFA Women's Under-17 Championship in Sweden with a 3-0 victory over Norway on 5 May 2024. Three days later, they thrashed hosts Sweden 5-1 as Isabelle Fisher grabbed a hat-trick in the triumph. England topped Group A with a 1-0 victory over France as Lola Brown's second competition goal proved decisive.

A commanding first-half display saw the WU17s 2-0 up after 34 minutes in their semi-final against Poland in Malmö. The 2-0 win set up a final against Spain at the Malmö Idrottsplats on 18 May 2024, in which the Young Lionesses were beaten 4-0.

MEN'S DEAF TEAM

England men's deaf team beat Germany 2-1 to secure a fifth-place finish at the 2024 Deaf Euros in Turkey. The Para Lions came away from the tournament in Antalya with a record of six wins from their seven games, with their only defeat coming against the host nation Turkey (0-2) in a hotly-contested quarter-final. France went on to beat Ukraine in the final of the competition.

2023 FA ENGLAND AWARDS

Here's how Three Lions fans voted in the 2023 England Men's and Women's Player of the Year awards.

HARRY
THIRD KANE

Captain of the national side since 2018, Harry Kane featured in 11 matches for England during what was a record-breaking season personally in 2022/23. Kane scored twice at the 2022 FIFA World Cup in Qatar – against Senegal in England's 3-0 win in the round of 16, and from the penalty spot as they went down 2-1 to France in the quarter-finals – to equal Wayne Rooney's record England goalscoring tally of 53.

Then, on 23 March 2023 the centre-forward made no mistake from the spot in a 2-1 win over Italy in a Euro 2024 qualifier to move ahead of Rooney and become the Three Lions' new all-time record goalscorer, with an astonishing 54 goals in just 81 matches.

Just weeks earlier Kane had also written his name into Tottenham Hotspur's history books, as his strike in their 1-0 victory over Manchester City on 5 February 2023 saw him surpass Jimmy Greaves to become the club's all-time top scorer with 267 goals. He departed N17 for Bayern Munich in the summer of 2023, having reaching a final tally of 280 Spurs goals.

An incredible debut season at the Allianz Arena in 2023/24 saw Kane net 44 times in 45 appearances, which included 36 goals in 32 Bundesliga matches. He was also in great form for England during the campaign. His eight goals included three at UEFA Euro 2024 which made him one of six joint-top scorers at the tournament along with Georges Mikautadze, Jamal Musiala, Cody Gakpo, Ivan Schranz and Dani Olmo.

JUDE
SECOND BELLINGHAM

Jude Bellingham's header to open the scoring for England in their 6-2 triumph over Iran in their first group game at the 2022 World Cup was his first senior international goal. And it wasn't his only goal involvement at the tournament, as the dynamic forward played a pivotal role in many of the Three Lions' attacking moves, and directly assisted Jordan Henderson for his goal against Senegal.

The Stourbridge-born player, who just keeps getting better and better, featured nine times for his country altogether during 2022/23 which included two UEFA Nations League matches against Italy and Germany, and he played all five games at the World Cup as England bowed out to France.

At club level, Bellingham's impressive performances for Borussia Dortmund in 2022/23 - as he netted 14 times in 42 appearances in all competitions - earnt him a raft of individual awards. He won the Bundesliga Player of the Season prize, the ESPN Midfielder of the Year award and was named the Golden Boy for 2023, an award made to the best male under-21 footballer playing in Europe's top leagues.

Real Madrid paid a reported £88m to sign Bellingham in the summer of 2023 and what a debut season he went on to have at the Estadio Santiago Bernabéu. He won La Liga, the Supercopa de España and the UEFA Champions League during the campaign, scoring 23 times in 42 matches. He netted twice for England at UEFA Euro 2024, including a memorable overhead kick against Slovakia to force extra-time in the round of 16 as the Three Lions eventually went on to the final.

BUKAYO
FIRST **SAKA**

Bukayo Saka netted seven times in 10 matches for England in the 12 months between August 2022 and August 2023. That included four games at the 2022 World Cup where he was named man of the match after scoring a brace in the 6-2 defeat of Iran on 21 November 2022. He also found the target during England's 3-0 win over Senegal.

Saka's fourth international goal of the 2022/23 season came against Ukraine in a UEFA Euro 2024 qualifier at Wembley Stadium on 26 March 2023. On 19 June that year, the Ealing-born player scored his first career hat-trick as he won his 28th England cap during another man of the match performance as the Three Lions beat North Macedonia 7-0 at Old Trafford, also in Euro 2024 qualifying.

The Arsenal Academy graduate was also a standout player for his club during 2022/23 as the Gunners finished as runners up to Manchester City in the Premier League. Saka netted 14 times and also made a number of key assists in 38 top flight games as he became the second youngest player in Arsenal's history to rack up 100 Premier League appearances that campaign.

At the end of the season, he picked up another individual accolade in the shape of the PFA Young Player of the Year award, while he was also included in the PFA Premier League Team of the Year and crowned England Men's Player of the Year connected by EE for the second time in a row.

A key performer for England during the 2023/24 season, Bukayo scored from long-range in the 1-1 UEFA Euro 2024 quarter-final draw with Switzerland. He then stepped up in the resulting penalty shootout to score in a 5-3 win, banishing the disappointment of his miss in the final of the competition three years previously.

THIRD
ALEX
GREENWOOD

A long-standing member of the Lionesses squad since making her debut in 2014, centre-back Alex Greenwood helped them make history by winning UEFA Women's Euro 2022. She featured in four games en route to the final and came off the bench in the 88th minute of the showpiece match at Wembley as they saw off Germany 2-1 in extra-time on 31 July 2022.

Sarina Wiegman continued to name Greenwood in her squads for World Cup qualifiers and friendly matches throughout 2022/23, and on 19 February 2023 Greenwood captained England in a 2-1 victory over Italy in the Arnold Clark Cup – a four-team competition they went on to win.

With the absence of Leah Williamson for the 2023 FIFA Women's World Cup, Greenwood shone in the centre of the Lionesses defence. She played in all seven of England's matches at the tournament and won huge praise for her performances as the team finished as runners-up to Spain who beat them 1-0 in the final.

The left footed defender won 17 caps for her country during 2022/23 and at club level, played 29 games in all competitions for Manchester City in the Women's Super League (WSL), whom she joined in September 2020.

Alex extended her England goal tally to seven during the 2023/24 season as she scored in the 2-0 UEFA Euro 2025 qualifying victory against the Republic of Ireland in Dublin in April 2024. She continued to be a consistent performer for City, netting once in 27 appearances during the campaign.

LUCY
SECOND BRONZE

More than nine years after making her England debut, Lucy earned her 100th international cap as the Lionesses took on the Czech Republic in a friendly on 11 October 2022. That summer Bronze had been a key part of Sarina Wiegman's team who became European Champions, starting all six games and netting in their 4-0 victory over Sweden in the semi-finals.

2023 began with Bronze being appointed a Member of the Order of the British Empire (MBE) in the New Year Honours for her services to association football. Back on the pitch, the versatile and athletic right-back was on the scoresheet in England's 6-1 Arnold Clark Cup victory over Belgium on 22 February 2023 en route to the team lifting the tournament trophy.

Lucy played all seven of the Lionesses' matches at the 2023 Women's World Cup, but sadly wasn't able to add 'World Cup Winner' to her long list of achievements as they were beaten by Spain in the final. She made a total of 16 international appearances during the 2022/23 season.

The 2019 Ballon d'Or Féminin runner-up has played for a number of clubs during her career including Liverpool, two stints with Manchester City, Lyon, Barcelona and in July 2024, Bronze signed for Chelsea. As was the case in her debut season, the attack-minded defender won the Supercopa de España Femenina, Liga F and the UEFA Women's Champions League in 2023/24 as well as the Copa de la Reina. She scored three times for England during the campaign with home and away goals against Scotland and one away to Belgium in the UEFA Women's Nations League.

MARY
FIRST EARPS

Mary Earps was an integral part of the Lionesses team during 2022-23, featuring in 16 international matches in total. That culminated in the Nottingham-born player winning the FIFA Golden Glove award for best goalkeeper at the 2023 Women's World Cup as England reached the final of the tournament and Mary saved a penalty from Spain's Jennifer Hermoso in the 68th minute of the showpiece match.

After playing a key role in their Women's EURO 2022 triumph, Earps was named FIFA's The Best Goalkeeper for 2022 at their awards ceremony in February 2023. The same month, she kept a clean sheet against South Korea and also played against Belgium in the Arnold Clark Cup.

On 6 April 2023, the shot stopper saved a spot-kick in a penalty shootout as England defeated Brazil in the inaugural Women's Finalissima.

More accolades followed for Earps, who signed for Paris Saint-Germain in the summer of 2024 after leaving Manchester United. She was named the 2023 BBC Sports Personality of the Year and in January 2024 won The Best Women's Goalkeeper once again, becoming the first two-time winner in the award's history.

CLASSIC MATCHES

The Three Lions have had some memorable matches. Let's look back at some of the best!

ENGLAND 4 WEST GERMANY 2 (AET)
FIFA World Cup Final
30 July 1966
Wembley Stadium, London

The 1966 FIFA World Cup was the first and, to date, only occasion England has hosted the tournament. It's also the only occasion the Three Lions have won it!

Back in '66, Sir Alf Ramsey's side topped Group 1 after a goalless draw against Uruguay and 2-0 victories over both Mexico and France. A Geoff Hurst goal saw the Three Lions edge a bad-tempered quarter-final with Argentina on 23 July 1966 before a Bobby Charlton brace helped England beat Portugal 2-1 at Wembley three days later in the semi-final.

Returning to the national stadium for the final against West Germany, England went behind after 12 minutes when Helmut Haller got to Ray Wilson's attempted clearance and struck past Gordon Banks in the England goal. But the 'home' side drew level six minutes later as Geoff Hurst scored with a header.

With 13 minutes of the 90 remaining, Martin Peters looked to have won the game for England as he turned home a deflected Hurst shot from around eight yards out. But failure to properly clear a West German free-kick resulted in Wolfgang Weber levelling from close range to force extra-time.

Hurst's second goal of the afternoon 11 minutes into the added period of 30 has long been a hot topic of conversation with the key question constantly asked... 'did the ball cross the line or not?' Crucially for England, linesman Tofiq Bahramov indicated to referee Gottfried Dienst that it had and the Three Lions regained the lead. There was no doubt about Hurst's hat-trick to seal the 4-2 win. The goal gave rise to one of the most famous commentary lines of all time as the BBC's Kenneth Wolstenholme remarked; "And here comes Hurst. He's got... some people are on the pitch, they think it's all over. It is now! It's four!"

ENGLAND 4 NETHERLANDS 1
UEFA Euro 1996 – Group A
18 June 1996
Wembley Stadium, London

Hosts of UEFA Euro 1996, England went on to reach the semi-finals of the 16-team tournament. The Three Lions' standout performance of the competition came in their final group match against the Netherlands. Terry Venables' team took the lead after 23 minutes of the match at Wembley, when Alan Shearer scored from the penalty spot. Six minutes into the second-half, Teddy Sheringham made it two as he headed in from a Paul Gascoigne corner. Sheringham teed-up Shearer for goal number three and then got on the end of Darren Anderton's spilled shot, to make it four. Patrick Kluivert got a late consolation for the Netherlands who qualified for the quarter-finals along with England.

GERMANY 1 ENGLAND 5
2002 FIFA World Cup Qualifying
1 September 2001
Olympiastadion, Munich

Having previously met at four World Cups and two European Championship finals, it's fair to say England and Germany had previous going into their 2002 FIFA World Cup qualification clashes in UEFA Group 9. Germany won the first of those games 1-0 in the last match at the 'old' Wembley Stadium in October 2000. Kevin Keegan resigned after that game and was eventually replaced as England manager by Sven-Göran Eriksson.

England trailed 1-0 to Germany after Carsten Jancker scored just six minutes into their September 2001 match. But the Three Lions levelled six minutes later through Michael Owen and went into the half-time break 2-1 up thanks to a thunderous Steven Gerrard goal. The second half saw Eriksson's men produce some scintillating football as Owen scored twice more to complete his hat-trick while Emile Heskey was also on target in the 5-1 win.

ENGLAND 2 GERMANY 1 (AET)
UEFA Women's Euro 2022 Final
31 July 2022
Wembley Stadium, London

Goalless at half-time, Sarina Wiegman made a number of substitutions during the UEFA Women's Euro 2022 Final that ultimately proved to be match-winning for England.

Along with her best mate and podcast co-host Alessia Russo, Ella Toone was introduced to the match on 55 minutes. Her impact was almost instant as, seven minutes later, she ran onto a through ball from Keira Walsh and lobbed the ball over Germany 'keeper Merle Frohms to give the Lionesses the lead.

Germany equalised 11 minutes from the end of the 90 as Lina Magull side-footed home at England goalkeeper Mary Earps' near post to force the game into extra-time. It was in the added period of 30 minutes that another of Sarina's super-subs delivered. On this occasion, it was Chloe Kelly who came off the bench to poke home the winner to give the Lionesses their first major tournament triumph.

SPOT THE DIFFERENCE

Can you spot the six differences in these photographs, showing England taking on Slovakia at UEFA Euro 2024?

WHO AM I?

Match these England players to the facts and test your knowledge of the teams.

PHIL FODEN

KEIRA WALSH

DEAN HENDERSON

MARC GUÉHI

HARRY KANE

DECLAN RICE

ALESSIA RUSSO

GEORGIA STANWAY

ELLA TOONE

LEAH WILLIAMSON

FACT 1
This goalkeeper holds two Guinness World Records titles. 'Fastest time to dress as a goalkeeper' (49.51 seconds) and 'most football headed passes in one minute' (91 – achieved with Jake Clarke-Salter).

ANSWER_____

FACT 2
This midfielder is nicknamed 'WonderWalsh' in reference to the Oasis song Wonderwall.

ANSWER_____

FACT 3
This defender once played piano along with a 57-person orchestra.

ANSWER_____

FACT 4
This defender was born in Abidjan in Ivory Coast.

ANSWER_____

FACT 5
This midfielder features on a popular podcast with England teammate Alessia Russo.

ANSWER_____

FACT 6
This midfielder is learning to be a tattoo artist.

ANSWER_____

FACT 7
This midfielder won three caps for the Republic of Ireland in 2018.

ANSWER_____

FACT 8
This forward is England's all-time record goalscorer.

ANSWER_____

FACT 9
This forward scored the Goal of the Tournament at UEFA Women's Euro 2022.

ANSWER_____

FACT 10
This forward won the BBC Young Sports Personality of the Year award in 2017.

ANSWER_____

Answers on page 60-61

CROSSWORD

Name England's opponents from the following clues to complete this crossword.

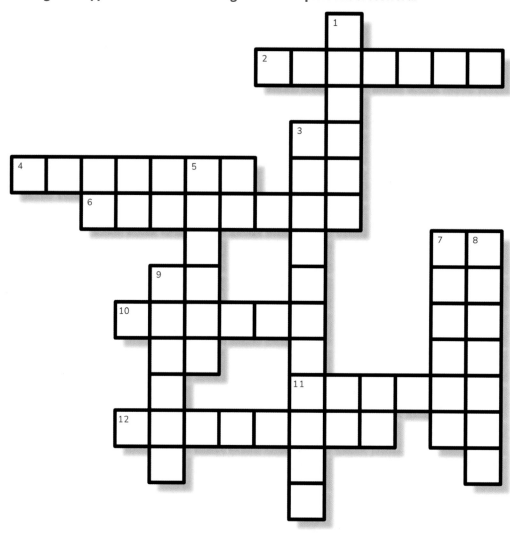

ACROSS

2. The team England Men staged a friendly against at Wembley Stadium just before Euro 2024 (7)

4. Nordic team who England Men faced in UEFA Nations League B Group 2 in September and October 2024 (7)

6. South American nation England beat on penalties at the 2018 FIFA World Cup (8)

10. Goals from Georgia Stanway and Alessia Russo saw England beat this team in Saint-Étienne in June 2024 (6)

11. The Lionesses beat this team by a record 20-0 scoreline in November 2021 (6)

12. England's 'Auld Enemy' (8)

DOWN

1. England's first opponents at UEFA Euro 2024 (6)

3. Hosts of UEFA Women's Euro 2025 (11)

5. Inflicted England Women's record defeat (0-8) in June 2000 (6)

7. Beaten on penalties by England in the 2023 Women's Finalissima (6)

8. England's opponents in the Women's Euro 2022 Final (7)

9. Surprise winners of Euro 2004, who England Men took on in the 2024-25 UEFA Nations League (6)

WORDSEARCH

Find the surnames of members of the England Men's Senior Squad in the below grid.

```
L N V G J Z O K N I Y P W D A P R I C E
W E K R A M S D A L E G D B D T E V B D
S H A W F K Y R P S D F A C A K S K O P
M U Z Z V K U X U D G R V L B T J X Z A
G U B U F A N V E U M R X T L Y E S F L
W P I E X N M Z E N H Y E V P A K Z W M
J T O M L E O O V K L K O A K N G X E E
F O D E N L N S A K A B J L L X H H N R
R H L G V B I Q K B O W E N J I Y B E X
U P T O L K E N Q F G B C Q S W S S V R
A F D L G M B N G U T O G Q P A W H T K
C V H T O N E Y P H O F M Y L T M P U Y
S K J N A N J Q K I A E V E L K M T C T
G T H O U I F G F B C M D O Z I M P Q I
S M O K X A Y W K T H K Q W E N S A N V
F V A N N Q N N A K Y I F U F S G H D N
I Z R I E D G S Q L O N K O W Z A V S B
A H G G N S Y B C M K O H X R T E X W I
R G Q L E O V X T V V E K B D D I Y W O
Q S N K O V O M O K O N R A W N A O R Y
```

DUNK	SAKA	RICE	TONEY
GALLAGHER	STONES	BELLINGHAM	WATKINS
GOMEZ	WALKER	FODEN	BOWEN
MAINOO	RAMSDALE	PALMER	EZE
PICKFORD	SHAW	KANE	GREALISH

Answers on page 60-61

ENGLAND QUIZ

Test your knowledge with 30 questions on various England teams...

1) Which stadium staged England's 3-0 victory over Bosnia and Herzegovina in June 2024?

2) Who was England's manager when they won the World Cup in 1966?

3) Which invitational tournament, hosted annually in the United States, did England Women win in 2019?

4) In which prestigious award was Lucy Bronze voted runner-up in 2019 and Beth Mead in 2022?

5) How many teams will compete at UEFA Women's Euro 2025?

6) Which national team did Sarina Wiegman manage between 2017 and 2021?

7) Who scored England's opening goal at UEFA Euro 2024?

8) Which club did Cole Palmer play for prior to signing for Chelsea in 2023?

9) Which city was Trent Alexander-Arnold born in on 7 October 1998?

10) Which club competition did Mary Earps, Maya Le Tissier, Katie Zelem and Ella Toone win in 2024?

11) Which stadium hosted the final of UEFA Euro 2020 and UEFA Women's Euro 2022?

12) Who is England Men's most capped player of all time?

13) ... And who is England Women's most capped player of all time?

14) In which English county is St. George's Park located?

15) Which country, along with England, Northern Ireland, Republic of Ireland and Scotland will host UEFA Euro 2028?

16) Including UEFA Euro 2024, how many European Championships have England Men appeared at?

17) What stage of the FIFA World Cup did England reach in both 1990 and 2018?

18) In which Australian city did England play their quarter-final, semi-final and final matches at the 2023 FIFA Women's World Cup?

19) Which stadium hosted England's UEFA Women's Euro 2025 qualifier against the Republic of Ireland in July 2024?

20) Who is the Lionesses' assistant coach?

21) Which former Manchester United and Everton player managed England Women between 2018 and 2021?

22) In which city was Kyle Walker born on 28 May 1990?

23) Who scored a hat-trick for England under-20s in a 5-1 win over Poland in March 2024?

24) In which African country did England under-19s play two friendly matches in March 2024?

25) Who scored England's goal in the UEFA Euro 2020 final of 11 July 2021?

26) What stage of the tournament did England reach at the 2022 FIFA World Cup?

27) Which forward was named England Men's Player of the Year for 2022-23?

28) Which goalkeeper was named England Women's Player of the Year for 2022-23?

29) Which Sheffield-based ground staged England's 4-0 UEFA Women's Euro 2022 semi-final victory over Sweden?

30) Which four-team invitational competition did England Women win in both February 2022 and February 2023?

Answers on page 60-61

ANSWERS

P54 SPOT THE DIFFERENCE

P55 WHO AM I?

1. Dean Henderson
2. Keira Walsh
3. Leah Williamson
4. Marc Guéhi
5. Ella Toone
6. Georgia Stanway
7. Declan Rice
8. Harry Kane
9. Alessia Russo
10. Phil Foden

P56 CROSSWORD

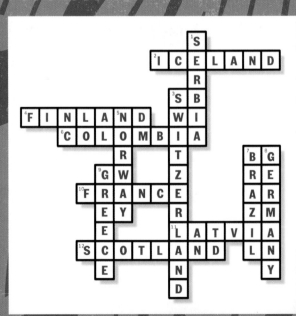

P57 WORDSEARCH

```
L N V G J Z O K N I Y P W D A P R I C E
W E K R A M S D A L E G D B D T E V B D
S H A W F K Y R P S D F A C A K S K O P
M U Z Z V K U X U D G R V L B T J X Z A
G U B U F A N V E U M R X T L Y E S F L
W P I E X N M Z E N H Y E V P A K Z W M
J T O M L E O O V K L K O A K N G X E E
F O D E N L N S A K A B J L L X H H N R
R H L G V B I Q K B O W E N J I Y B E X
U P T O L K E N Q F G B C Q S W S S V R
A F D L G M B N G U T O G Q P A W H T K
C V H T O N E Y P H O F M Y L T M P U Y
S K J N A N J Q K I A E V E L K M T C T
G T H O U I F G F B C M D O Z I M P Q I
S M O K K X A Y W K T H K Q W E N S A N V
F V A N N Q N N A K Y I F U F S G H D N
I Z R I E D G S Q L O N K O W Z A V S B
A H G G N S Y B C M K O H X R T E X W I
R G Q L E O V X T V V E K B D D I Y W O
Q S N K O V O M O K O N R A W N A O R Y
```

P58-59 ENGLAND QUIZ

1) St. James' Park

2) Sir Alf Ramsey

3) SheBelieves Cup

4) Ballon d'Or Féminin

5) 16

6) Netherlands

7) Jude Bellingham

8) Manchester City

9) Liverpool

10) The Adobe Women's FA Cup

11) Wembley Stadium

12) Peter Shilton

13) Farah Williams

14) Staffordshire

15) Wales

16) 11

17) Semi-final/third place play-off

18) Sydney

19) Carrow Road (home of Norwich City)

20) Arjan Veurink

21) Phil Neville

22) Sheffield

23) Dane Scarlett

24) Morocco

25) Luke Shaw

26) Quarter-finals

27) Bukayo Saka

28) Mary Earps

29) Bramall Lane

30) The Arnold Clark Cup

SPOT THE PLAYERS

Can you spot the three Lions and three Lionesess hiding in the crowd at UEFA EURO 2024?